EXPLORING SPACE

ROCKETS

BY DALTON RAINS

WWW.APEXEDITIONS.COM

Copyright © 2024 by Apex Editions, Mendota Heights, MN 55120. All rights reserved. No part of this book may be reproduced or utilized in any form or by any means without written permission from the publisher.

Apex is distributed by North Star Editions:
sales@northstareditions.com | 888-417-0195

Produced for Apex by Red Line Editorial.

Photographs ©: Joel Kowsky/NASA, cover; Brandon Hancock/NASA, 1, 26–27; Kim Shiflett/NASA, 4–5, 9; NASA Photo/Planetpix/Alamy Live News/Alamy, 6–7; NASA, 10–11, 16–17, 18, 19, 21, 22–23; Shutterstock Images, 12–13, 24, 29; NACA/NASA, 14–15

Library of Congress Control Number: 2023910084

ISBN
978-1-63738-740-5 (hardcover)
978-1-63738-783-2 (paperback)
978-1-63738-868-6 (ebook pdf)
978-1-63738-826-6 (hosted ebook)

Printed in the United States of America
Mankato, MN
012024

NOTE TO PARENTS AND EDUCATORS

Apex books are designed to build literacy skills in striving readers. Exciting, high-interest content attracts and holds readers' attention. The text is carefully leveled to allow students to achieve success quickly. Additional features, such as bolded glossary words for difficult terms, help build comprehension.

CHAPTER 1
FALCON HEAVY 4

CHAPTER 2
EARLY ROCKETS 10

CHAPTER 3
INTO ORBIT 16

CHAPTER 4
LATER ROCKETS 22

COMPREHENSION QUESTIONS • 28
GLOSSARY • 30
TO LEARN MORE • 31
ABOUT THE AUTHOR • 31
INDEX • 32

CHAPTER 1

FALCON HEAVY

A rocket blasts off from the Kennedy Space Center in Florida. It is a Falcon Heavy. The large rocket has three **boosters**. Their engines shoot out hot gas.

A Falcon Heavy rocket launched on February 6, 2018.

Two of the Falcon Heavy's boosters fire their engines as they return to Earth.

After a few minutes, two of the boosters separate. They descend back to Earth. The boosters land safely on the ground.

REUSABLE BOOSTERS

The Falcon Heavy's boosters have a way to land safely. Near the ground, the boosters fire their engines. That slows their fall. Legs extend for landing. Then they can be reused on future missions.

Later, the third booster separates. The **payload** continues on to space. A new **satellite** begins to **orbit** Earth.

FAST FACT

The third booster lands on a platform. The platform floats in the ocean.

Elon Musk founded SpaceX. This company built the Falcon Heavy rocket.

CHAPTER 2

EARLY ROCKETS

Rockets use controlled explosions to move. Early rockets were small. People used them as weapons. But some people hoped to send them to space. They made new parts and fuels to do this.

The first rockets were used in China during the 1200s CE.

Germany fired more than 3,000 V-2 rockets during World War II.

Rockets improved during World War II (1939–1945). For example, V-2 missiles were made in Germany. These rockets carried strong explosives. They killed many people.

FAST FACT
V-2 missiles could go about 200 miles (322 km).

Scientists kept developing new rockets. They became more powerful. Some rockets helped scientists study high up.

US scientists test a rocket in 1957.

CONTROLLING ROCKETS

In the 1900s, scientists invented ways to control rockets. They added **fins** to keep rockets stable. Some rockets used smaller rockets on the side to steer. Others could move their engines to steer.

CHAPTER 3

INTO ORBIT

Rockets first reached orbit in the late 1950s. They began bringing satellites and people into orbit.

The first US rocket in orbit launched in 1958. The Soviet Union sent one to orbit just months before.

STAGES

Many rockets have several stages. One stage burns its engines until the fuel runs out. Then, it splits off from the rocket. After that, the engines on the next stage fire.

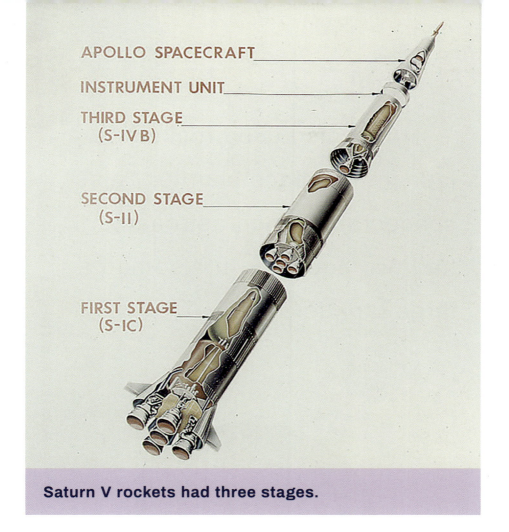

Saturn V rockets had three stages.

NASA built the Saturn V rocket. It was used in the 1960s and 1970s. It helped bring humans to the Moon.

◀ The first launch of a Saturn V rocket happened in 1967.

NASA also used rockets to launch the space shuttle. This spacecraft carried astronauts. It had two boosters. It also had a large tank for fuel.

FAST FACT
The space shuttle's boosters landed in the ocean. Then they were reused in later launches.

The space shuttle was the first spacecraft that had reusable parts.

CHAPTER 4

LATER ROCKETS

In the 2000s, companies designed many new rockets. Some were reusable. These rockets use engines and **landing gear** to return to Earth. Later, they can fly again.

Workers recover a rocket booster in 2005.

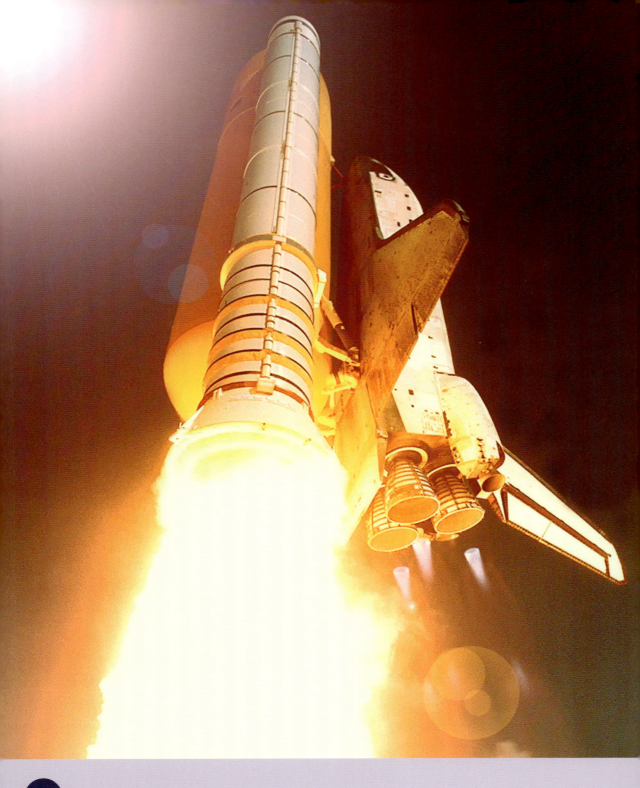

New rockets launch satellites. They also carry people. Some bring crews to the International Space Station (ISS). Eventually, scientists and companies hope to send people to other planets.

FALCON 9

In 2010, SpaceX launched its first Falcon 9 rocket. This rocket is reusable. By 2023, there had been more than 200 Falcon 9 launches.

Rockets reach speeds of more than 4.9 miles per second (7.9 km/s).

In 2022, NASA launched a new rocket. It was called the Space Launch System. It was the most powerful rocket ever.

FAST FACT

Some companies send **civilians** to space. People pay money to travel to the ISS or orbit Earth.

NASA designed the Space Launch System to carry very heavy loads.

COMPREHENSION QUESTIONS

Write your answers on a separate piece of paper.

1. Write a paragraph that explains the main ideas of Chapter 3.

2. Which rocket would you most like to fly in? Why?

3. When did rockets first reach orbit?
    - A. the 1200s
    - B. the 1950s
    - C. the 2000s

4. Why might reusable rockets be helpful?
    - A. They take longer to build and are much more expensive.
    - B. Scientists do not have to build new rockets for every launch.
    - C. The materials used to construct them are safer.

5. What does **developing** mean in this book?

*Scientists kept **developing** new rockets. They became more powerful.*

    A. improving
    B. landing
    C. destroying

6. What does **descend** mean in this book?

*They **descend** back to Earth. The boosters land safely on the ground.*

    A. spin
    B. rise
    C. fall

Answer key on page 32.

29

GLOSSARY

boosters
The first stages of rockets or rockets that fire for a short time.

civilians
People who are not part of the military or a space agency.

fins
Flat parts of rockets that stick out to help control movement.

landing gear
The part that holds an aircraft or spacecraft up when it is on the ground. Landing gear helps with landing and taking off.

NASA
Short for National Aeronautics and Space Administration. NASA is the United States' space organization.

orbit
To follow a curved path around an object in space.

payload
The cargo or passengers in a vehicle.

satellite
A device that orbits Earth, often to send or collect information.

TO LEARN MORE

BOOKS

Morey, Allan. *Exploring Space*. Minneapolis: Bellwether Media, 2023.

Murray, Julie. *Rovers*. Minneapolis: Abdo Publishing, 2020.

Stratton, Connor. *Space Exploration*. Lake Elmo, MN: Focus Readers, 2023.

ONLINE RESOURCES

Visit **www.apexeditions.com** to find links and resources related to this title.

ABOUT THE AUTHOR

Dalton Rains is an author and editor from Saint Paul, Minnesota. He loves to learn about new science discoveries.

INDEX

B
boosters, 4, 7–8, 20

E
engines, 4, 7, 15, 18, 22

F
Falcon 9, 25
Falcon Heavy, 4, 7–8
fins, 15

I
International Space Station (ISS), 25–26

K
Kennedy Space Center, 4

N
NASA, 19–20, 26

O
orbit, 8, 16, 26

S
satellites, 8, 16, 25
Saturn V, 19
Space Launch System, 26
stages, 18

V
V-2 missiles, 13

W
World War II, 13

ANSWER KEY:
1. Answers will vary; 2. Answers will vary; 3. B; 4. B; 5. A; 6. C